P9-EFJ-974

WORRY

how to feel less stressed
and have more fun

by Judy Woodburn and Nancy Holyoke
illustrated by Brenna Vaughan

Published by American Girl Publishing

No part of this book may be used or reproduced in any manner whatsoever without written permission except in the case of brief quotations embodied in critical articles and reviews.

19 20 21 22 23 QP 13 12 11 10 9 8 7 6 5 4

Editorial Development: Darcie Johnston
Art Direction and Design: Jessica Rogers
Illustrations: Brenna Vaughan
Production: Jeannette Bailey, Virginia Gunderson, Mary Makarushka, Cynthia Stiles
Special thanks to Jane Annunziata, Psy.D.

This book is not intended to replace the advice or treatment of health-care professionals. It should be considered an additional resource only. Questions and concerns about mental or physical health should always be discussed with a doctor or other health-care professional.

Library of Congress Cataloging-in-Publication Data
Woodburn, Judith, 1959-
A smart girl's guide, worry : how to feel less stressed and have more fun / by Judy Woodburn and Nancy Holyoke ; illustrated by Brenna Vaughan.
    pages   cm. — (A smart girl's guide)
Audience: Age 10+
ISBN 978-1-60958-745-1 (pbk. : alk. paper) — ISBN 978-1-60958-764-2 (ebook)
1. Stress management—Juvenile literature. 2. Stress management for children—Juvenile literature. I. Holyoke, Nancy. II. Vaughan, Brenna, illustrator. III. Title.
RA785.W66 2016   155.9'042—dc23   2015024830

© 2016, 2018 American Girl. All rights reserved. Todos los derechos reservados. Tous droits réservés. All American Girl marks are trademarks of American Girl. Marcas registradas utilizadas bajo licencia. American Girl ainsi que les marques et designs y afférents appartiennent à American Girl. **MADE IN CHINA. HECHO EN CHINA. FABRIQUÉ EN CHINE.** Retain this address for future reference: American Girl, 8400 Fairway Place, Middleton, WI 53562, U.S.A. **Importado y distribuido por** A.G. México Retail, S. de R.L. de C.V., Miguel de Cervantes Saavedra No. 193 Pisos 10 y 11, Col. Granada, Delegación Miguel Hidalgo, C.P. 11520 Ciudad de México. Conserver ces informations pour s'y référer en cas de besoin. American Girl Canada, 8400 Fairway Place, Middleton, WI 53562, U.S.A. **Manufactured for and imported into the EU by:** Mattel Europa B.V., Gondel 1, 1186 MJ Amstelveen, Nederland.

americangirl.com/service

Dear Reader,

Do you tend to worry about things? If so, you're not alone. Experts say that at your age many girls start to worry a lot. They worry about friends and fitting in. They worry about their grades, their looks, and their families. They may even worry about whether they worry too much!

Everybody worries, and sometimes it's a good thing. But other times worry is like a faucet that won't turn off. Worries just keep coming. You don't feel like the girl you want to be, because you're forever fighting your fears, thinking, *What if . . . ? What if . . . ? What if . . . ?*

But what if you knew how to handle your worries? What if you were able to reassure yourself when they bubble up? What if you could stop some before they even start?

You can—and this book will show you how. Here you'll find quizzes and tips to help you learn more about your-self—and how worry really works. You'll learn tricks to help your body feel calmer. You'll hear from other girls about how they've handled their worries. You'll get real help on dealing with your hardest feelings and facing your worst fears. You'll also find ideas for chilling out when you're stressed and moving on when you make mistakes.

The world will never be worry-free, but worries don't have to hold a girl back. We hope this book gives you just what you need to feel a little calmer and more confident every day—so that whatever you dream of doing, there won't be a worry in the world that can stand in your way.

Your friends at American Girl

contents

all stressed out

I probably
spend half my
life worrying.
—Savannah

tied up in knots

Worries. We all have them. Some are mild. Some are strong. Sometimes they show up one by one. Other times they may start pouring in so fast you think there's nothing you could ever do to stop them.

What if they laugh when I sing?

The reports are due tomorrow. Mine's going to be the worst.

What if my friends fi

What if I can't finish my report?

What if I can't make

What if I speak up and hurt my friend's feelings?

What if a boy asks me out?

What if the plane crashes?

What if I miss the kick and we lose the game?

Nobody's doing anything about global warming!

What if I freak out?

What if I ra

What if my friends laugh at my haircut?

What if I get unpopular?

What if they get mad at me?

I did finish my bibliography. Didn't I?

What if I get a C on my test?

What if I drop my note cards?

If I can't get ratios, I'll never get in honors math.

my stuffie?

What if I cry at the overnight?

Will Mom be safe on her business trip?

What if my best friend dumps me?

r my new school?

What if I can't remember my locker combination?

Call it nerves, call it anxiety, or call it being stressed out. When worry has you tangled up in knots, it may seem as if no one could possibly understand how it feels.

What if I'll have to run extra laps with everybody watching.

What will it be like after Mom and Dad's divorce?

What if my new glasses look horrible?

Do I have taco breath?

What if a man with a gun breaks in?

What if Mom loses her job? Or Dad? Will we have enough money?

What if lightning hits the house?

If I'm late, I'll have to run extra laps with everybody watching.

d give the wrong answer?

What if I get fat?

What if this is germy and I get sick?

What if I can't stop worrying!?!

What if I throw up in front of the class?

Not so. There are girls all around who know exactly how it feels because the truth is, a lot of girls struggle with worry.

why all the worry?

Experts say kids worry more these days than in the past. It's not hard to see why.

Life is packed.

School, piano lessons, soccer matches, clubs, mathalons, performances, family events. You're forever rushing off to do the next thing. Chances are, even if you're alone in your room, things are hopping. Phones ring. Texts ping in. Nothing ever settles down. It's hard to relax.

The pressure's on.

School is more demanding. There's more homework, more classes, more teachers—and more pressure to do well. And that's not to mention the pressure to do well in sports and other areas of life. *Argh!*

Life is changing.

Friendships can be complicated. There's more drama, more gossip, more tension in the lunchroom. At the same time, your body is changing. The "you" you are today may not feel at *all* like the one you were last year. Lots of girls worry about what comes next. *Will my breasts start growing soon? What if my period starts in the middle of dance class?* Your body will do exactly what it's supposed to, but it will have its own unpredictable timetable.

Your world is getting bigger.

You are building your independence. More and more, you're venturing out of the cozy cocoon your parents watched over when you were little. You're deciding more things for yourself. It's exciting, but a bit scary. You're not always certain what to do.

Things feel less safe.

Weather disasters, wars in distant countries, unsafe schools. Bad news can be worrisome even for adults. For kids who are just beginning to pay attention, it may be plain scary. What kind of world are you stepping into anyway?

There are always problems.

Of course, there are plenty of things closer to home that a girl might have good reason to worry about, too. One girl may have a loved one who's sick. Another may be anxious about arguments in the family. Money problems. Marriage problems. It's a lucky girl who doesn't have at least some family concerns on her list. And as if that weren't enough . . .

Worry can be contagious.

If adults or others around her tend to worry about things, a girl can pick up the worry habit. A girl whose aunt shrinks from meeting new people, or whose dad is too frightened to fly on airplanes, might learn to be anxious—not only about those specific things but about other things, too.

Add it up.

A day has only 24 hours, but for a lot of girls that means a bajillion opportunities to worry about *something*.

when you worry

Anxiety is normal. It's your brain and body's built-in alarm system, and it has only one job: to protect you. Back when humans wore animal hides and lived in caves, this alarm system helped your ancestors escape from hungry animals.

When something sets off the alarm, anxiety gets you ready to . . .

fight back   or   **freeze so you won't be noticed**   or   **run away.**

To do this, anxiety affects you in three ways.

1. Anxiety focuses **your thoughts** on the danger. *I've got to get away!* Suddenly, you can't think of anything else. Not. One. Single. Other. Thing.

2. Anxiety revs up your body and changes **how you feel.** Your heart beats faster and your muscles tense up. Is your skin sweaty? Is your stomach tied in knots? Do your legs feel like rubber bands? That's anxiety at work, too.

3. Anxiety can affect **what you do** in an instant. A heartbeat ago, you were strolling through the woods, humming along to your favorite song. And now you are . . . *running like crazy!*

The anxiety alarm can still kick in even if you're not fleeing wild animals. An ordinary thing like a visit to the dentist can set it off if you're worried enough. And the science test Mr. Baake is giving—the one that counts for a third of your grade? Or the party that your karate teammate is throwing—where you're sure you won't know a soul? Those could trip the alarm, too.

Anxiety is your own personal bodyguard. It rallies to keep you safe from anything that's scary to *you*.

go, fight, win!

No girl likes the way she feels when she's worried or afraid. But anxiety isn't *all* bad.

When worry focuses your thoughts, it can help you zero in on anything that's really important at home or school. When it revs up your body, it can give you a burst of energy.

The good thing about worry is that it can push you to do what needs to get done.

Get busy!

Stay focused!

Do your best!

So when you're worried, maybe you can put those feelings to use. Try asking yourself: "What, exactly, is nagging at me? Is there something I can do about it?"

If you feel like you ate a bowl of butterflies two days before the Spanish vocabulary quiz, that feeling might be telling you to put away your MP3 player and get out the flash cards. That headache you get whenever you think about your piano recital or a swim meet might be reminding you to practice a little more, try a little harder.

If there's something you *can* do about what's worrying you, the surest cure is to just do it. Now. If worry can get you going, it's on your side.

out of control

The problem comes when worry spins out of control. Here's how it works: Our thoughts create our feelings. Then our feelings lead to actions, and those actions create more thoughts. It's a loop. In stressful times, anxiety can take hold and build on itself till it takes on a life all its own.

See how it works? Anxious thoughts make you feel scared, sad, and ashamed. The situation seems hopeless, so you don't do anything to change it. That leaves you feeling worse, only now your worries may be even stronger because they've been running the show since you first thought "what if?" It's a vicious cycle.

How can this all play out?

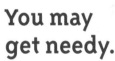

You may get crabby.

It's hopeless. You've spent a half hour on *one stupid problem*. What if you can't get any of the others either? What if you flunk the class? If your stupid brother weren't playing that noisy video game, you'd be able to think. You start yelling at him. Again.

You may get needy.

"Can you help me pick out my outfit? Do I look OK? Can you find my gloves for me? I can't get this zipper. Can you do it? I can't decide what to pick. Will you pick for me? I need—"

"Sweetie," says your dad, "you need to do a few more things by yourself."

You may feel sick.

It's the second week of school, and once again you can hardly get out of bed. Your head aches. You're dizzy. You're exhausted. Do you have a fever? No. But if you so much as think about leaving the house, you end up in the bathroom getting sick in the sink.

You get trapped by your fears.

"My sister's taking me horseback riding," says Maggie. "Want to come?" *Horseback riding!* That would be so much fun! But what if you're no good at it? What if you fall off? What if you get hurt? "Sorry," you say, "I have to study."

You can't stop criticizing yourself.

"Great job," says your teacher. "You played that beautifully." Was she even listening? What about the wrong note you played in the fifth bar? The performance is this weekend, and you're going to stink.

You can't have fun.

"That was the best movie *ever*," says LaToria as you leave the theater. Was it? You wouldn't know. You spent the entire show wondering why Simon hasn't answered your text. Did you say something stupid? What if he's sharing it?

You can't stop worrying.

You're going on vacation. Yay! Only . . . did Dad put your bag in the car? Did Mom lock the door? What will the hotel be like? What will you eat? What if you get lost? What if the cat— "What if you stopped asking questions for once?" says your brother.

In other words . . .

When worry has its way, life becomes complicated, exhausting, and unhappy.

So, do girls sit back and say, "Whoa. Something has to change here. Worry is taking over my life"?

Some do, but some don't. That's because worry is sneaky. Worry is tricky. Worry stirs up all these difficult feelings and then ducks the blame.

The truth is, it can be hard to recognize that it's worry, and not something else, that's the real problem. For some girls, feeling angry, queasy, and stressed out may start to feel natural. They start to believe this is just who they are. They think, *Maybe this is just how life feels. Maybe this is just what life's all about.*

It's *not* what life's all about.
It's what *worry* is all about.

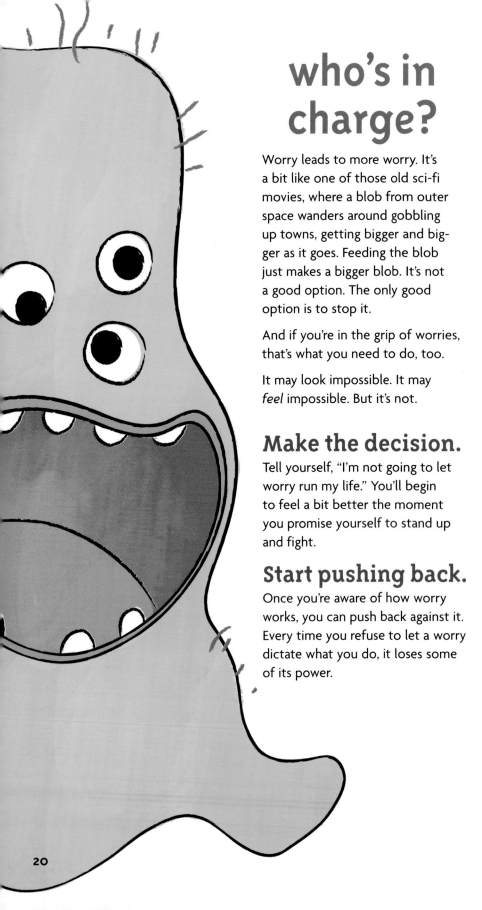

who's in charge?

Worry leads to more worry. It's a bit like one of those old sci-fi movies, where a blob from outer space wanders around gobbling up towns, getting bigger and bigger as it goes. Feeding the blob just makes a bigger blob. It's not a good option. The only good option is to stop it.

And if you're in the grip of worries, that's what you need to do, too.

It may look impossible. It may *feel* impossible. But it's not.

Make the decision.

Tell yourself, "I'm not going to let worry run my life." You'll begin to feel a bit better the moment you promise yourself to stand up and fight.

Start pushing back.

Once you're aware of how worry works, you can push back against it. Every time you refuse to let a worry dictate what you do, it loses some of its power.

Keep at it.

Taming worry is a skill. You can master it just like you learned to ride a bike, multiply numbers, and whistle. It won't happen overnight, but it doesn't have to. All you need to do is keep at it. Do that, and you'll start seeing things more accurately. Your days will be happier, and eventually your worries will shrink to a size that's easier to live with.

look who's talking

I worry about a LOT of things all the time. To calm myself down, I talk to myself in my head.
—Sandy

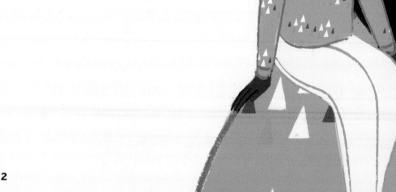

the inside story

Worries often feel as if they start outside you and work their way in. But do they? Experts say that anxious feelings aren't caused by what actually happens. Instead, they're caused by how you *think* about what happens. Let's say two girls are about to take the same geography test. Who's going to have a stomachache before it's over?

Thoughts like these can zip in and out of your head so fast you might not even notice you're thinking them. What you *do* notice is how they set you up to feel. Some thoughts lead to feeling relaxed and in charge. Other thoughts leave you feeling overwhelmed before you even start.

The trick to feeling better begins with knowing one simple fact about your thoughts:

You don't have to listen to them, because they aren't always true.

If you worry a lot, it's a sure bet that many of the thoughts popping into your head aren't accurate. They may actually be fooling you into worrying. Mistakes can happen in your thinking just as they can happen when you're baking. It's easy to grab the wrong container and pour in salt instead of sugar. You might not even notice your mistake—at least at first. But *blech!* One taste of the cookie will tell you that something went wrong.

Luckily, you can start to catch your thinking mistakes before they turn a whole day sour with worry. When you know what to look for, mistakes are easy to spot.

worry words

When you hear these words inside your head, it's a red flag. Your worries are talking, and you're right to be suspicious.

never

always

no one

can't

nothing

should

everyone

impossible

supposed to

ought to

have to

shouldn't

Worries that spread

If you allow a goal in gym class, do you automatically think that other things will go wrong, too?

> Now *nothing* will go right.
> I *always* mess up.

If friend A is mad at you, are you convinced that friends B through Z are mad, too?

> *Everyone* thinks I'm wrong!
> *No one* takes my side!

Thoughts like these let a problem in one area of your life spill over into places where it doesn't belong. To fix this mistake, try drawing a mental line around the problem. Tell yourself: "Just because I didn't play well today doesn't mean I won't do OK on the math quiz."

All-or-nothing thinking

> It's *impossible* to finish this assignment.
> Leila *never* sits with me.

All-or-nothing thoughts like these can really supercharge worries. Chances are, the truth is less black and white. An assignment might not be easy, but it's probably not impossible. And maybe Leila sits with Carmen on Wednesdays because they've just had gym together, just as she sits with you on Thursdays after the two of you get out of band. Try to find the middle ground. Using words like "sometimes" (instead of "always" or "never") or "challenging" (instead of "impossible") can help you think about things in a less stressful way.

Rules and more rules

> I *have to* get all A's in English.
> I *should* have learned a handspring by now.

Rule-bound thoughts tell you there's only one way for you to be OK. They tell you that if things don't happen exactly the way they're supposed to, it will be a disaster. If that were true, who *wouldn't* worry? The truth is that you're still learning and growing, discovering who you are and what you can do. There are an infinite number of ways things can go and still turn out right for you. Go easier on yourself by thinking about your goals in a gentler way. "I'd like to . . ." "I want to . . ." "It would be nice if . . ." are great places to start.

shady characters

Worry disguises itself in all kinds of ways. Have any of these shady characters ever paid you a visit?

The oracle

She knows what's going to happen in the future—or she pretends to anyway—and it's always bad.

The judge

Did something go wrong? There might be dozens of other people involved, but day in, day out, the judge puts the blame on a single one: you.

The psychic

Even though it's impossible to read minds, this guy somehow always knows what other people are thinking about you—and it's never good.

The name-caller

The meanest kid at school isn't as cruel as this gal.

The sorcerer

His spells transform the tiniest problem or imperfection into a catastrophe.

The mad scientist

She's got a ray gun that blasts good news to ashes. Did you do better than before? *Zap.* Did you learn something new? *Zap.* Did someone give you a compliment? *Zap.* Doesn't matter, doesn't count, who cares.

All these voices aim to make your life as miserable as possible. So when one of them shows up in your head, just say, "No thanks, I'm not buying this," and push it right back out.

reality check

When you worry, put those thoughts to the test. Ask yourself, "What proof do I have that these thoughts are true?" Look for ways to get more accurate information about what's worrying you.

NO ONE is going to come to my Halloween party tonight!

Hmm. "No one" is pretty strong. What are the facts? People came to my birthday party two months ago . . .

But Rosa didn't come. And she wasn't sick because I saw her in school. She thinks I have boring parties.

There are lots of reasons Rosa might not have come. Maybe her mom couldn't drive her. Maybe that's the weekend she had to go to her dad's. There's no reason to blame myself.

But Rosa and Madison barely talked to me today at lunch. They must be mad at me. Maybe they will talk other people into not coming.

Wait. I can't know what they're thinking. I'm not a mind reader! Maybe they didn't have time to talk because they were busy with Future Problem Solvers. And I'm not a fortune-teller. There's no way I can know they won't come.

There's no way I can know anyone WILL come either!

Well, most kids have RSVP'd. And I could just call and ask the others if they plan on coming.

31

Bust worries by reminding yourself that things can still be OK if they don't go as planned. You can also try imagining that you're giving advice to a good friend who has the same worry. Finally, try to paint a clear picture in your mind of how things will go better if you *don't* worry.

If I call my friends, I'll have a realistic idea of who's coming.

But I'm too nervous to call and ask people if they're coming! What if someone says no?

Well, I can prepare myself for that by expecting a few "no"s. Some kids probably have other plans. "No" doesn't mean a girl doesn't like me. "No" just means she can't come.

Everyone simply HAS to come or it will be a total flop.

That's all-or-nothing thinking, which usually isn't true. It would be nice if everyone could come. But a party with 6 kids can be as fun as one with 12.

Only for losers.

Wow. If my friend was worried about her party, I wouldn't call her a name like that. I would try to help her not to worry.

If I don't worry, I might forget something or make a mistake!

That thought doesn't make any sense! I've already fixed the snacks and planned the games. It doesn't help me at all to worry now.

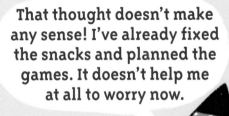

Yes, it does! Worry keeps me from being surprised by something awful.

No, it doesn't. We'll all have a lot more fun if I'm not a ginormous ball of stress.

Maybe you're right, but . . .

There's only one way to find out! I can't wait for tonight!

Mmphhmglmmm . . .

33

keeping worries in their place

Here are some more tricks to try. Every girl is different, so keep experimenting until you find the strategies that work for you.

Think in threes.

When that worried voice in your head is predicting a disaster, get out a pen and paper—*quick!*—and jot down three different ways things could go. Are you afraid you'll have an awful time on the ski outing because your best friend isn't going? Your list might look like this:

1. I could try to sit with Luis or Reina on the bus. I don't know them very well, but I usually like talking with them.

2. There are 44 kids signed up. Maybe I will meet someone new.

3. Even if I ski mostly alone, I might have an OK time. I have fun biking by myself.

If you can think of more than three things, keep writing! Worry has a way of focusing you on how things could go wrong. Your list can open you up to all the ways they can go right. With luck and practice, you may find yourself looking forward to something you were dreading.

Find a better use for "but"s and "if"s.

Worriers use these little words a lot: "But what if something awful happens?" Instead, try turning "but" and "if" *against* worries. Whenever a worrisome thought springs up, use these words to add another thought, to see things in a more realistic way.

I might forget my lines during the play . . . **But** I've worked hard to memorize them, and I did OK at the dress rehearsal. **If** I have trouble, Ms. Gerace will whisper a cue.

Make a date with worry.

It seems nutty, but planning to worry can help you keep anxiety corralled. Tell yourself you absolutely *must* worry every day for, say, 15 minutes after you get home from school. Then do it. Set a timer and *really* worry. Write down every single worry you come up with. Then, when the timer goes off, put the list away. When a worry comes up, tell yourself, "I can think about that tomorrow at 2:55. I don't need to think about it now." Having a plan for worry can help you feel more comfortable with letting anxious thoughts go.

Hello, worry!

Once you've gotten some practice challenging your worries, you may find you can let some of them come and go in your head without having to talk back to them at all. When the same old worry visits you, you might picture it as a bubble that rises in a glass of cola, and then—*pop!*—fizzles away. Or you could imagine that the worry is someone you recognize in the hallway. Say, "Oh, hello again, worry! Sorry, no time to talk today!" Then waggle your fingers and keep right on going.

pressures &
perfection

I feel as if I need to make everyone else happy all the time. I want my parents to be proud of me, but it's just too much pressure. Feeling that I need to be perfect really stresses me out.

—AG Fan

not good enough

Worry taps into some very big feelings that live within us all.
Could this be you? Answer the questions.

1. "Does anyone have anything to add?" says Ms. London. *You do! You do!* But the other kids might not be as into wolves as you are. What if everybody thinks you're dumb? Your hand stays in your lap.

a. could be me

b. not likely

2. "Let's make cottage cheese for our report," says Tiana. Of all the topics on the list, "Explore cottage cheese" is your least favorite. But if you disagree, Tiana might think you're a bad partner. "OK," you say.

a. could be me   **b.** not likely

3. The popular boys sit at the front table at lunch and make comments to girls as they walk by. You start going around to the back hallway so that you can come in by the kitchen.

a. could be me

b. not likely

4. Uh-oh. Mr. Weill picked you for the solo. You love to sing, and you've got a good voice. But what if you screw up?

a. could be me   **b.** not likely

5. You and Josh are doing a layout for the yearbook. "What about this?" he says. You think you have a better idea, but you don't want to be bossy. "Sure," you say.

a. could be me

b. not likely

6. "STUDENT COUNCIL ELECTIONS THIS FRIDAY" says the poster. First you think: *Cool. Maybe I'll run.* But then you think: *Will my friends think I'm full of myself? What if I lose? I'm not really a leader anyway.* You decide to skip it.

a. could be me

b. not likely

Answers

If you answered with a lot of **a's,** your doubts are affecting your life in a big way. It's hard to act freely because you're thinking: *Will I seem mean? Will I make a mistake? How will I look?* Dig a little deeper, and you'll find one very big, very bogus idea: *I'm not good enough.* How do you bust an idea that seems to be such a part of you?

You defy it, that's how. You picture what an unworried girl would do in situations like these, and you do that, whether it feels comfortable and safe or not. You raise your hand when it scares you. You sign up even if you're afraid to lose. You do what you want to do, despite your worries. By pretending to be brave, you'll find you really *can* be brave. You'll discover your strengths. You'll learn to trust yourself. Most of these worries will fall away, and the idea that you're somehow worth less than other kids will go with them.

the need to please

Let's talk about "nice."

Most of us like the idea of being a nice person. We want to be nice to others. It just seems like the right thing to do. We may also figure that if we're nice to others, they'll be nice back—and wouldn't that be nice! Nice is good. Nice is nice! Who would argue with that?

Well, maybe you should. Being kind, being respectful—that's part of being a decent human being. And doing certain things you don't want to do (like cleaning the house) is just being responsible. But there are other ways in which a lot of girls worry too much about pleasing other people. They worry about being liked and included at school. They worry about disappointing their friends and parents. So they put a smile on their face and try to be agreeable about everything.

Along the way, words that express a different point of view . . .

I'd like   I think   **I disagree**   I don't want

I'm not   I want   No

. . . begin to feel "not nice." A girl may end up operating as if she had no right to express how she feels at all.

Where does this leave her? Too often, in places she doesn't want to be, doing things she doesn't want to do. Not to mention the fact that the harder a girl tries to please others, the less she likes herself.

So try these thoughts on for size.

You don't like every person you meet. It doesn't mean you *dis*like them. You're just not interested in spending time with them. That's natural. It's just as natural that there will be people in this world who aren't so interested in you. Everyone's different. We're drawn to different things, and that includes people. So you don't need to stress out about making everyone like you. It's not possible.

But there are plenty of people who *will* like you, and it won't be because you've earned their approval by doing what they want. They'll like the way you laugh, the way you see the world. They'll like you because they enjoy being with you.

Of course, a girl may know this and still find "Sure" coming out of her mouth before she's had a chance to think about it. So don't operate on automatic. Give yourself time before you answer when you're sitting around the lunch table with friends. Ask yourself, "What *do* I think? What *do* I want?" Act on that.

Does this mean others will be disappointed? Sometimes. But ask yourself: "Am I worth less than other people? Does what I want always have to come last?" Surely the answer is no. You want to be a generous, giving friend, and, yes, there will be times you give up something you want for others, and that's fine. But you don't want to be so "nice" that you end up feeling fake—and angry because you get so little of what you yourself truly want. So remind yourself: It's not your job to make other people happy. They have to find happiness on their own, just as you do. Your job is to grow up happy with yourself.

6
risks every girl should take

#2 Take helpful feedback.

Your coach is telling you how you could have prevented the other team's goal. You hate hearing it, but you listen.

What you'll discover: Life gets a whole lot easier when you can take criticism. Criticism is a part of life. If you teach yourself how to learn from it, that's going to keep your mind open and your skills sharp. It builds confidence, too, because you're telling yourself, "I'm strong enough to take this."

Would you like to feel more confident? Take a few small trips outside your comfort zone. You'll be amazed how different the world looks from there!

#1 Voice a different opinion.

Your friends think Mr. Nuckles is the worst teacher in school. But you like him. You say so.

What you'll discover: It feels good to say what you think. People respect that. It shows strength, and it's honest. A girl who can express her point of view is going to end up far happier with herself, and far less anxious, than a girl who has to look around the table before she opens her mouth.

#3 Dare to stand out.

You want to be president of the Robotics Club, so you put your name on the ballot.

What you'll discover: Ambition is good. It means you want something and are willing to go after it. That's healthy. You're teaching yourself to own your strengths.

#4 Say no.

Your friend really, really wants you to go to the mall. You don't want to. You say no.

What you'll discover: You don't have to agree with everything and everybody to be liked. You can say no when you want to. It's freeing to know that. And it relieves a lot of anxiety about doing things you don't want to do.

#5 Be direct.

Saskia has had your bracelet for weeks. You consider saying, "Sorry, but could you maybe return my bracelet? I was thinking I might like to wear it again." Instead you say, "I'd like my bracelet back, please. Could you bring it tomorrow?"

What you'll discover: You can stop apologizing. People will understand you better. Being polite doesn't require you to muffle everything you say in packing pellets.

#6 Ask for what you want.

There are three parts in the play: a girl, a troll, and a toaster. You want to be the toaster. You say so.

What you'll discover: It's not selfish to say what you want. It doesn't mean you're greedy. You're just plain saying what you want. You may not get it, but at least you let people know. How will you ever get what you hope for in the world if you're scared to acknowledge what it is?

What you'll discover in all of this: Taking small risks can make you more confident. It's a way of experimenting with your fears. Every time you say what you think and your world doesn't fall apart, you'll feel a little less worried about speaking up the next time.

bff's

Anger and worry often show up hand in hand.

Mom will be gone for 2 weeks!?!?

You may find yourself fighting with your mom about homework because **you're freaked out** that she's leaving you and going away on a trip.

You may be so worried about your new haircut that **you blow up** when your brother moves your nail polish off the sink.

I look like a cactus!

When you're mad about a situation, you're probably **anxious about how to respond** to it.

What will I do?

You may be more nervous about the choir trip because **you had a fight** with a friend before you left.

My stomach feels awful. I'm so tense!

Plus, **anger is just sort of scary.** When you're furious, you may be worried you're going to lose control and ball yourself into a wad of tension to prevent it.

In the end, worry and anger may get so thoroughly mushed up together that you can't tell them apart. But here's some help for handling the unhappy superpowers of this dynamic duo.

Watch for signs.

Notice when you're tense. Are you talking louder and faster? Do you feel jumpy and jittery? These are signs that your emotions are building. It's time to slow down and think.

Locate the worry.

Ask yourself: "What is it that really matters here? What's truly wrong? What do I want? Why? What am I afraid of? Where's the anger actually coming from?"

Question blame.

The thought arrives red-hot and lightning fast: *It's all their fault!* And that could be. But when you feel attacked or wronged, it's good to double-check your response. Ask yourself: "What role is fear playing in all this? How would I see things differently if I weren't afraid? Is there something here that I need to open up my mind to and understand?"

Say what's what.

When you realize that worry has made you blow up, say so.

> I'm sorry. I'm just really nervous that you're going away. I'm going to miss you!

> I'm sorry. I'm upset about this stupid haircut. But I also really don't like it when you move my stuff.

Let it out.

You may be justifiably angry about something but still scared about how you feel—and *really* scared when you think about what to do. So sit down with someone you love and trust, and say that. Let it all out. A sympathetic listener will help you feel clearer and calmer. She can also help you decide what to do next.

45

how to be mad

A lot of girls worry about expressing anger, especially with their friends. It makes them nervous, so they get locked into a bunch of reasons they can't do it. In fact, a girl can learn to express anger the same way she can learn to do anything else. So let's bust a few myths about getting mad.

Myth 1
It wouldn't be nice.

Anger isn't mean, and it isn't shameful. It comes with the disagreements that are part of all relationships. A girl can learn to express anger respectfully, and it's important she do so. If she doesn't, those feelings will come out some other way—often in dramas, backstabbing, and gossip. *That's* what's not nice.

Myth 2
It won't help.

Actually, it can. When you're mad, you're unhappy with a situation. Telling a friend how you feel is a chance to change things. It's your chance to explain what's wrong, how you feel, and what you'd like to happen. That's how problems get solved.

Myth 3
If it doesn't work, it'll be a disaster.

All conversations won't end with a hug, that's for sure, but that doesn't mean an uncomfortable one is a disaster. When you have a conversation like this, you're saying, in one way or another, "This isn't OK with me. This has to change." The other girl may reject that message while you're talking, but she'll remember it. Down the road, good things could still come from your honesty.

Myth 4
I can't say how I feel. It's impossible.

It's not impossible. You just need to plan ahead. What do you want the other girl to know about how you feel? What do you want her to do? Set some goals. Write it all out. Then write out the words you'll use, too. Don't attack or accuse ("You walked off laughing with Lauren. You were so mean!"). Instead, talk about how things seem to you ("When you walked off with Lauren, I felt hurt. I was worried you were laughing at me"). After you've written down what you want to say, do something else for an hour, then come back and reread everything. Is it fair? Accurate? Change the words till you get it right. Finally, practice what you want to say in front of a mirror. The words will begin to feel natural, and you'll feel more confident.

Myth 5
She won't listen.

Could be. Chances are, she's got some fears of her own. If she feels defensive, her first response could well be anger. But if you stick with the plan, and talk about how things look and feel to you, that's going to help. It will also help if you express feelings other than anger. You can tell her, "I was afraid to talk to you." You can say, "I'm worried that our friendship is ending" or "I was ashamed of what I said the next day." By opening up, you help her feel safer to do the same. Of course, you also have to be ready to listen— really listen. You have to be prepared to hear how things seem to *her*.

the girl in the mirror

When you were little, you made faces in the mirror, tried on goofy costumes, and giggled like crazy. Now, for many girls, looking in the mirror ends up being a search for what's wrong. *Am I pretty? Am I getting more freckles? Is this shirt out of style?* And the more you check to make sure things are OK, the more you find to worry about. It still feels crazy, but not in a *good* way.

Please, please don't call on me. Why didn't I finish the assignment instead of taking selfies all night? And why can't I get just ONE where I don't look like a hamster when I smile?

What did Ms. Bjurlin just say about flaming alcohol burners? No clue. All I can think about is this pimple on my chin. It's probably grossing out the whole class.

I weighed two pounds more this morning than I did last week. I'm never eating pizza again.

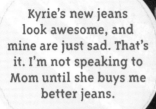

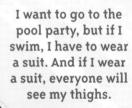

Kyrie's new jeans look awesome, and mine are just sad. That's it. I'm not speaking to Mom until she buys me better jeans.

I want to go to the pool party, but if I swim, I have to wear a suit. And if I wear a suit, everyone will see my thighs.

So if we do it right, the hot soda can crushes itself? Cool!!

It's a rare, lucky girl who doesn't worry—at least a teensy bit—about her looks. Most girls *do* struggle with the mirror. Sometimes these worries multiply until a girl believes there's something wrong with her body or her style and that people will judge her for it. If that happens to you, just wanting to look your best becomes a trap. It keeps you from having fun and steals your time and attention from things that really matter.

Feeling confident in your body means seeing past what movies, TV, and the Internet tell you about how girls should look. It means seeing yourself as a whole person—a girl with skills, interests, and dreams that have zero to do with her hair, her skin, her stomach, or her clothes.

how do I look?

Ready to break free of body worries?
Here's where to start.

Don't believe the image.

You've heard it before, but it's worth hearing again: Most celebrity photos involve special lighting and truckloads of makeup. They've been retaken countless times and tinkered with afterward. If it's a photo of someone you know, it's the one lucky shot where everything happens to look better than normal. Real-life bodies just aren't perfect, period.

Put away the magnifying glass.

Almost every girl has some part of her body she'd like to change. The "problem area" can get magnified in your head until you feel downright defective—until you feel as if it's the only thing others notice about you. The truth? No one will ever judge your "flaws" as harshly as you do. They are too busy worrying about their own.

Focus on the positive.

Confident girls know to focus on what they like about their bodies, not what they don't. What do *you* love about your looks? Is it your million-watt smile? Your strong legs? The way you look in hats? When you're feeling uncertain, remind yourself that *every* body has pluses and minuses . . . then give yourself a compliment for the pluses.

Be a friend to your body.

If a friend fed you, carried your books, walked your dog, wrote your assignments, and did a million other things for you every day, would you call her names? Would you criticize her? Your body makes practically everything in your life possible. Try showing your appreciation by using kind words when you think or talk about your body. Send it a little message of thanks right now!

Move . . . and move some more.

Using your body is the key to feeling comfortable in it. You walked five miles and raised money for charity? You scored a three-pointer in basketball? You cook wicked pancakes on Sundays? Fantastic! The more you enjoy whatever your body can do, the less you will worry about how it looks.

Stay off the scale.

Unless a doctor tells a girl to weigh herself, there's absolutely no need for her to do it. The number on the scale is just that—a number. It has nothing to say about how pretty you are, how likable, or how good you are at anything.

Take back your mirror.

OK, you're not going to stop looking in mirrors. But a mirror check can become a reality check. Tape reminders on your mirror of what's really important to you—a favorite poem, a photo of the penguin you help sponsor at the zoo, or a goal you've set. Anything will work if it reminds you of the truth: You are *far* more than that girl in the glass.

less than perfect?

Do you worry about being less than perfect? Answer the questions.

1. "And first place goes to . . . " Not you.

   a. You think, *Oh, well. I'll try again next year.*

   b. You're really disappointed, but by dinnertime you're over it.

   c. You're crushed. How could you have submitted such a stinky, rotten, horrible entry? People must think you're an idiot.

2. You take the cake out of the oven and flip it over to get it out of the pan. *Plop.* It falls in half. You . . .

   a. moosh the halves together and ice the thing. You'll have some fun telling the story when you serve it.

   b. fit the halves together and make a second batch of icing to cover up the crack. No one will ever know!

   c. throw everything away and start over.

3. Corrine's family does a weird sport called curling. "Want to try it sometime?" she asks.

   a. You say, "Sure."

   b. You say, "I'll probably stink, but OK."

   c. No way are you doing something new when you don't know if you'll be good at it. You say, "No thanks."

4. You've been the top scorer ever since you started to play. Before a game you feel . . .

   a. pumped and confident.

   b. nervous.

   c. sick to your stomach. What if this is the day you make a mistake?

5. Your friends all know that your room . . .

   a. looks like a hurricane hit it.

   b. is the place to hang out.

   c. is off-limits. You don't like people in there, messing it up.

6. Everyone's doing posters for the school carnival. Most kids finish in an hour. You finish . . .

   a. in an hour.

   b. in two hours.

   c. You don't. Two days later, you're still trying to get the lettering to look like it came out of a printer.

7. Instead of a quiz, Mr. Lugnut is going to have a trivia contest. All the kids say you're going to win. You feel . . .

   a. flattered.

   b. nervous.

   c. angry. Being you is too much pressure.

Answers

If you got lots of a's, you operate as if mistakes are part of life and learning. That lets you adjust to setbacks and helps you stay confident.

If you got lots of b's, you try hard to do well, but if you're not perfect, that's OK. At the end of the day, you're satisfied with you.

It's good to be good at things. It's good to try hard to do things right. But if you got lots of c's, anything less than perfect means heartbreak. No matter how often you come out on top, you still get up every day worried about falling short. It's a tough way to live. Since there's no such thing as a perfect person, you're destined to wear yourself out. So tell your inner critic to knock it off. Dump the "must"s and "should"s. Be kind to yourself. You'll find that being imperfect is a happier, healthier way to be.

10
perfectly terrific reasons to ditch perfection

1. Setbacks make you stronger.

A girl who never fails never gets the chance to figure out how to bounce back. Bouncing back—picking yourself up and trying again—builds grit. That's a kind of strength you can't get any other way.

2. Flubbing can make you kinder.

If you know how it feels to mess up, you can be a more understanding friend when things go wrong for someone else.

3. Mistakes show you're making progress.

It sounds backward, but it's true. When you're learning something new, mistakes are part of the process. If you're not making any mistakes, it means you're not pushing the limits of what you're *already* good at.

4. When you fail, you find things out.

Failing tells you what doesn't work. That's often the best way to figure out what *does*. The authors rewrote this page four times before they came up with an idea that worked!

5. Chocolate-chip cookies

6. Potato chips

7. Ice-cream cones

Here's a fun historical fact: All of these fabulous treats were invented by accident, when cooks ran out of ingredients or just messed up a recipe. What might *you* come up with if you let go of insisting that everything be Just Exactly Right?

8. Flaws make life more fun.

A girl who's not busy protecting a perfect image will find it much easier to relax and enjoy other people. Others will have more fun with her, too. Friendships bloom best when others can see who you are—flaws and all.

9. You'll worry a lot less if you fail a little more.

A girl who's bent on perfection harbors big, worrisome questions: "Will I be OK if I mess up? Will anyone like the real, imperfect me?" The answer, of course, is yes. But the only way you know it for certain, deep in your gut, is if you fail and find out.

So why not practice being imperfect— on purpose?

Think disaster awaits if you don't study three hours for a test? Set a timer and close your book after one or two hours instead. Reveal a flaw to a friend. Wear mismatched mittens. Don't know all the steps? Dance anyway. Do it, and feel the relief.

P.S. The authors made a mistake on this page on purpose. Have fun finding it!
(See page 95 for the answer.)

facing your fears

If you can just take that first big step, it gets easier to face a fear.

—Hope

meet the avoider

You're worried about a certain something. Logic says you'd be happier if you dealt with it somehow. But if you're like most people, what you really want to do is run the other way. We all know how *that* works.

You procrastinate.

I have to finish all my reading first.

I have to clean my room.

I have to fold my socks, and dust my pencils, and sort my hats.

I need a snack first.

I'll do it after I finish this game, and watch this show, and answer this text.

My hamster needs me.

My goldfish needs me.

I'll do it when I'm ready. I'll do it tomorrow, or next week, or next year.

You may create distractions.

You pick a fight, create a drama, or have a meltdown.

You pretend to be sick.

Or you stress yourself out so much you really *do* get sick.

You may make up excuses.

They'll never agree to that anyway. There isn't time anyway. Nothing's going to help anyway.

On second thought, I'm fine.

You may deny there's a problem at all.

When you avoid your fears, your first feeling may be *Whew! What a relief!*

Yay! I didn't have to do the thing I dread!

But you won't feel relieved for long because your fear is still there, right where you left it, in the middle of the road—only now it's bigger and more powerful than it was before. What's happened?

For one thing, you're teaching yourself that your fear is too big to be challenged. You're teaching yourself that you're helpless, and missing out on the chance to prove you're not. Plus, the brief relief you feel is a reward you're giving yourself for procrastinating. It makes you more inclined to do it again. The result?

The more you avoid a fear,
the more impossible it will feel to do anything else.

That's why avoidance is no kind of solution for a girl who's miserably anxious about something. The solution is to do the opposite. The solution is to face that fear and conquer it.

"no way!"

Face your fear? Your first response is likely, "No way!" It can be hard enough to keep your fear under control. Why would you want to get it all riled up by challenging it? Even thinking about it may make you sick, and it probably makes you mad.

You hate how you feel. You hate the control your fear has over you. You may be blaming yourself for not being like the kid at the next desk, who seems to have no fears at all. You probably believe that other people don't understand what it's like for you, and you're probably right. They don't.

> Do people think I WANT to feel this way? I'd face my fear if I could. But that's asking too much. I can't DO it.

That said, there must also be a big part of you that wants all this to stop. So look at it this way.

Right now, your fear is like a mountain of dirt sitting in the doorway. You can no more move it aside than you can grow wings and fly to Brazil. It's too much. But what you can do is move a little bit of it. Not a lot. A cupful. A handful. A pinch. Whatever you can manage. Then you can do it again. And again. And again.

That's how change works. It's slow, but it's real.

When it comes to fears, this means you start by doing something that scares you only a little bit. Maybe you do it again. And again. You do it until you know you can handle it. Then, when you're ready, you do something that scares you a bit more. Then, again after a while, when you're ready, you do something that scares you a bit more than that.

In other words, you don't try to face your fear all at once. You divide it up. This is a system developed by experts, and it works. You'll read about it in the following pages. It's going to let you move mountains.

Is it hard to imagine? Yes. But think about it. You've been moving mountains one cup at a time all your life. You're a pro. Exhibit A: You weren't reading books like this the first day you opened your eyes. You learned your letters one by one. You learned words the same way. You practiced. There were probably moments when you thought, *This is hard. I can't do it*. But you didn't let that stop you. You kept plugging away. You got more confident. You got better at it until reading just became part of you.

You can master a fear in much the same way. Attack the problem bit by bit, and the mountain starts to shrink until at last the way is clear. You'll find blue skies ahead.

getting ready

When you're getting ready to go somewhere or start a new activity, it's important to take along the things you'll need. It's the same with facing your fears. Before you begin, you'll want to have some tricks like these to help you keep your cool.

Take a deep breath.

Why do people always say "breathe" when someone's tense? It's because your breathing gets fast and shallow when you're nervous. Switching to deep, slow breaths can help change the body chemistry that keeps anxious feelings going. It really does help you feel better. So pause. Count to 4 in your head while you take a slow breath in through your nose. Let your belly swell out as you take in air. Then count to 4 again as you breathe out through your mouth. Do this several times. *Ahhhhhhhh.*

Give yourself a squeeze.

Muscles clench up automatically when you're stressed. It's hard to get a tense body to relax by just ordering it to, but you can *trick* muscles into letting go. Start with your feet. Curl your toes and squeeze hard. Keep squeezing! Now let them relax. Move on to your leg muscles. Squeeze for a bit, and then let go. Keep moving up your body, squeezing the muscles in your hips, belly, hands, arms, chest, and face. Each time you release the squeeze, you'll feel a little more of the tension melt.

Focus on now.

When you worry, you focus like a laser beam on horrible things that might happen next: *Will I drop my nunchucks in the karate tournament? What if I fall off the ski lift?* Help your brain tune in to the present instead: Make a mental list of absolutely anything you can hear right this moment. A car starting? Wind in the trees? The way your teacher says his S's? Or observe things you can feel with your body: Is your seat hard or soft? Can you smell a marker pen, or someone's perfume? Can you feel the cool air passing through your nose as you breathe? Carefully noticing what's really happening will help take your mind off what you think *might* happen.

Psst!

One of the best things about these tricks is that people can't tell when you're using them. You don't have to put your hands in funny positions, breathe loudly, close your eyes, or do anything that looks out of the ordinary.

The idea is to practice these tricks before you need them so that it feels natural to use them when you're stressed. Why not try them out right this minute— wherever you happen to be? No one will know!

I want to go to weekend sleepaway camp with my friends, and I want to have a great time.

getting set

What would you do if worry weren't calling the shots?

If just the thought of being away from your parents makes your insides icy, a goal like going to camp may seem crazy, even unreachable. It's not. You'll get there just the way you get every-where else: one small step at a time. What you need is a plan. Here's how to make it.

First, name the worries that are getting in your way. They might be:

I hate being away from my parents.
I'm scared I'll need my mom.
I worry that something bad will happen.
I'm afraid I won't be able to sleep.

Then make a list of situations when you feel those worries. Here's what a girl who gets anxious when she's away from her family might include:

Hearing my friends talk about camp.
If my parents are upstairs while I'm downstairs.
When I'm hanging out at someone else's house.
Slumber parties away from home.

Next, rank each situation for how worried it makes you on a scale of 1 to 7. A 1 is something you don't like doing but you can do it, and a 7 is so terrifying that your heart races and you get upset just *thinking* about it.

Now put the situations in order, from least to most scary. If you've rated two things the same, toss a coin to decide which to list first.

You're almost done. Come up with ways to practice being more com-fortable with each situation on your list. For example, to practice being comfortable alone upstairs, try doing it for just a few minutes to start.

Last, write your goal. Now you have a face-your-fears plan.

You can create a path with just a few steps, or with lots of steps, depending on what feels comfortable for you. Here's an example.

Step 1: Check out the camp website and ask other kids what it's like. **1**

Step 2: Stay downstairs 5 minutes while Mom and Dad are upstairs. **3**

Step 3: Hang out at a friend's house for an hour. **3**

Step 4: Stay home while Mom and Dad run an errand. **4**

Step 5: Hang out at a friend's house for the day. **6**

Step 6: Stay at a friend's house until bedtime. **6**

Step 7: Spend the night at a friend's house. **7**

Camp Hav-a-Blast, here I come!

Now you can see a path that leads where you want to go.

steady as you go

OK. You've got a path for facing your fears.
You've practiced your relaxation tricks.
Now it's time to take that first step.
Then the next. And the next.

At each step, talk back to your worries if they start to bother you. Use your relaxation tricks to help keep your mind and body steady. Keep repeating each step until you feel yourself starting to get used to it.

With practice, each time will feel less and less scary. It will start to feel, well, almost ordinary. When that happens, it's time for the next step. Each time you move along your path, you can expect to gain a bit more skill at worry-busting.

What if it still feels scary?

Don't expect the fear to disappear completely—at least not right away. Each step on your path is something new, and it's totally normal for new things to feel weird or stressful at first.

If the fear gets too intense, or if it feels like you're moving too fast, you can back up a step and practice more before moving on again. Or you can make the next step easier. You can . . .

Adjust the steps.
Not ready to take a certain step? Add another step or two to make your path more gradual. If you can't stand being near spiders, look at a photo of one. That can help prepare you for the real thing. If you can't believe you'll be able to go out on a high balcony, try imagining it. Preparing your mind really can help!

Get a partner.
Do a step with a friend or parent by your side before you try it solo. Need more support? Ask a parent or counselor to help you find a therapist. A therapist knows how to help people plan steps and work their way through them.

Use a timer.
Plan to do a step for just a short time—maybe 30 seconds, maybe 5 minutes, depending on what it is. For later steps, you can gradually increase the time.

Change the time of day.
It might be easier to try some steps during the day before tackling the same steps at night.

Remember: This is *your* plan. You're in charge. The right pace is the one that allows you to keep moving forward.

With each step, you're making progress. You're winning out over worry and fear. You've got more control. Your thinking is clearer, less gummed up by worry messages. You're getting better and better at this.

So flex those muscles. Feel how strong you're getting!

lucky charms

Some kids find it easier to face a fear if they're wearing a lucky pair of socks or earrings or have a lucky charm tucked in a pocket. But the best lucky charms are the ones you'll never be without, because they are a part of *you*.

Your patience

When your body's on red alert, it's an actual physical workout. Your body can't keep this up for very long, so sooner or later the panicky feeling runs out of "juice" and goes away. Knowing this can help you face any really intense feeling. Tell yourself, "This feeling can't hurt me. It won't last forever. It will pass."

Your imagination

Change the scary channel in your mind by imagining something nice. Picture yourself under a shady tree with a glass of lemonade, in a bubble bath, or curled up on the couch with your cat. Anything you picture is great, as long as it's warm and safe.

Your memory

Have you memorized the theme song of your favorite television show? Do you know all the state capitals by heart? Can you remember the number pi out to 24 digits? In a super-anxious moment, reciting poems, songs, math problems, or facts in your head can keep your mind off your fears.

Your inner voice

When it has calming things to say, that little voice inside your head is a powerful force against worry. Make a list of statements that encourage you, remind you of your tools, and leave you feeling in charge. You can write each statement on its own little card, clip the cards together on a key ring or large paper clip, and carry the set with you until you remember the phrases by heart.

I have what it takes to get through this.

Breathe deeply and feel more peaceful.

I won't let worry win here.

Sing my song.

Worry feelings always pass.

I don't have to feel completely calm to keep going.

Whisper my poem.

I can wait until 4:30 to worry about this.

There are LOTS of ways things can turn out OK.

Change the channel in my mind.

Relax my shoulders and my face.

Picture my dog playing with me.

I don't have to be perfect.

checking in

Whew! Time to take a breath and congratulate yourself for doing what you're doing.

Celebrate

When you've done something hard, take a moment and reward yourself. Sit under a tree and watch the clouds go by. Reread the last chapter of your favorite book. Put on some music and dance through every room of the house. Stand on your head and wiggle your toes. Celebrate! You deserve it.

Setbacks

There will be times when you don't accomplish what you set out to do. It's all part of the process. When you feel you've taken a step backward, ask yourself what situation triggered this strong response. This is a chance to understand your fears better and think up more steps to get past them.

Getting unstuck

There may also be times when you just feel stuck—and in an odd way, deep down, you may be OK with that. You may find yourself thinking, *This is just how it is. I belong where I am.* It's almost like you're choosing to worry. And maybe you are.

However unpleasant worry is, it can give a girl some benefits. She may get extra attention. She may not be expected to do what others do. There may be some privileges she would have to give up if she stopped worrying, and some responsibilities she'd have to take on. All this means you might want to ask yourself if a part of you actually prefers to worry.

What does worry get you? What does it cost you? Make two lists. Then take a good look at them and see which one speaks to the bright spot in your heart.

WORRY GETS ME
More attention
I don't have to make changes
Fewer responsibilities

WORRY COSTS ME
Pride
Confidence
Happiness
Fun opportunities

Sticking with it

Worries are like weeds. You can pull them up in May, but if you totally ignore your garden, they'll grow back by June. So hold on to your successes by repeating them. Redo your steps as often as you can. Make them the new normal.

New goals

You can map out a plan for any fear or worry. If you have more than one fear, make more than one plan. As always, if you need ideas, ask a parent or another trusted adult for help.

My goal: Dive off the diving board at the pool

Step 1: Watch other kids diving. 1

Step 2: Practice jumping off the side of the pool in the deep end. 2

Step 3: Stand on the diving board and bounce a little. 4

Step 4: Practice diving off the side of the pool in the deep end. 4

Step 5: Jump off the board without bouncing. 5

Step 6: Bounce and jump off the board. 6

Step 7: Bend down and dive off the board. 7

1 2 3 4 5 6 7

brave girls talking

Every girl who's faced a big fear started out thinking it was impossible. Here's what some girls like you have had to say about what happens next.

I learned that thinking about facing a fear is worse than actually doing it.
—Chelsea

You don't really know how something will turn out until you try it.
—Emma

What helped me was taking it one step at a time. That let me ease myself back into confidence.
—Mindy

I told myself, "Other people do this every day, so I probably can do it, too." I thought this a couple of times, and then I just did it. It was awesome!

—Lila

At first I could not get over my fear. But then I tried again and again. Finally, I found that I wasn't as scared as before. I still get nervous. But I just take a deep breath and say I can do this, and I do.

—Bridget

I was so afraid. I felt like I would faint. But then I reminded myself I really wanted to do this, and that my family and friends would all be there for me. That helped a lot.

—Lizbeth

Sometimes you just have to say yes.

—Camille

taking charge

Sometimes life
seems like too
much to handle.
—Halyna

dazed & crazed

A lot of stress comes from how we live our lives.
Could this be you?

1. Breakfast was two bites of cereal. Lunch was French fries and a cookie. Dinner is fresh stir-fry, but you're not that hungry because you scarfed down two sodas, a bag of chips, and a bowl of ice cream when you got home from school.

a. Yes, that's pretty much me.

b. No. I try to eat three full meals, so I don't get snack attacks.

2. Your report is done, it's fabulous— and it's lost. Is it under the laundry on your desk? At the bottom of your backpack with last year's cough drops? No one's seen the floor of your closet for years, so it better not be in there. *Argh!* Why do you keep losing things?

a. Yes, that happens to me a lot.

b. No, I usually know where stuff is.

3. Chores, homework, practice. You've got to do it all. Before you start, you deserve to relax with a TV show. Or two. So you do. The problem is that when you get up from the sofa you feel worse than you did when you sat down.

a. Sounds familiar, yes.

b. I do that sometimes, but not a lot.

4. You're working on a geometry problem—and listening to music, watching TV, answering texts from Jasmine and Anuj, and keeping a chat running with Erin.

   a. Yes, that's my style.

   b. No. I try not to do too many things at a time.

5. You're in soccer, swimming, debate, Scouts, karate, band, class council, Computer Club, Spanish Club, Pottery Club, Book Bunch, Future Zookeepers, Singmaniacs, Bug Lovers, and drill team. How do you do it? Simple: You don't rest, eat, exercise, or sleep.

   a. Yes. Sigh. That would be me.

   b. No. I'm busy, but I've still got some downtime.

6. If you had to describe your life in one word, it would be . . .

   a. Crazed

   b. Busy

Answers

If you had lots of **a's,** you're living with some serious stress. If you had lots of **b's,** you aren't. The difference comes from some basic choices. What you eat is a choice. Whether you exercise is a choice. How much you pack into your schedule is a choice, and so is how you manage your time. Make those same choices again and again, and they begin to feel so normal that you forget there's a choice involved at all.

But there is. So when you're feeling crazed, remind yourself that there's a lot here you can control. If you make a few different choices each day, you can start forming new, healthier habits. Little by little, life will get happier and a whole lot more relaxed.

10 ways to cut the stress

Who has the most control over the stress in your life?
You do. You can start using it now.

1. You can slow down.

Do things one at a time. Get dressed first, then eat, then text, and *then* hunt for those mittens. Don't try to do everything at the same time. Slow it down. It's amazing how much calmer things seem when you stop rushing.

2. You can eat healthy.

A car can't go very far on a gallon of gas, and a human body can't go far on a bowl of neon breakfast cereal, either. Soda, candy, and junk food just don't have much nutrition. Your body needs fresh fruits and vegetables. It needs whole grains, protein, and milk. Eat healthy, and your body and mood are healthier.

3. You can exercise.

Ride your skateboard around the park. Walk to your friend's instead of asking your parent to drive you. Get out the door and move! Science shows that exercise releases a chemical that literally makes a person feel better. Exercise also helps you relax. It keeps your body strong and energetic. Plus, you're building skills that make you proud.

4. You can get organized.

It's crazy-making to always be tearing around the house looking for your favorite shirt. So get organized. Drop your bus pass in the same spot when you come in. Have a special place for your homework. Putting things away in the same spot means you'll know where to find them when you need them. Organize your time, too, by keeping a calendar. Is there a test next week? When's the recital? Write it down. Before you go to bed at night, pack your backpack for the next day. A little planning goes a long way to making life more manageable.

5. You can do the tough stuff first.

If you're surfing the net when you'd planned to be studying for the Spanish test, are you having fun? Not likely, because the test is a big black cloud in the back of your head. Procrastinating is stressful. If you study last, you're worried all night. It's only when you do the tough stuff first that you truly get to relax.

6. You can cut back on commitments.

It's good to be involved, but a kid who's frazzled and exhausted 24/7 is a kid who's doing too much. Drop a few activities, and you'll enjoy the remaining ones a lot more.

7. You can limit screen time.

Looking at a screen gets your brain hopped up, and nonstop texting makes it tough to concentrate on anything at all. Calm it down. Put a limit on screen time, and enjoy the people you're with.

8. You can schedule downtime.

Everybody needs a time to relax—to take a break from all the things we do in a day, and from the screens that demand our attention. So make sure you get yours. Write a story or paint a picture. Find a shoelace and play with the cat. Take a warm bath. Or just close your eyes, send your brain on vacation, and practice your calming skills.

9. You can stay in touch.

Hug your parents. Call a friend. Find things to laugh about, and when you need help, ask for it. Stay in tune with the people you love.

10. You can be thankful.

Keep a list of all the things you're thankful for. Give yourself sweet dreams by writing down one new thing every night before you climb into bed.

making decisions

Should you buy the blue coat or the gray one? Should you go to the sleepover or the dance? Should you try advanced math? Making decisions can get you spinning. Here's how to stop.

Should I play the clarinet or the drums?

Start by doing some research. Ask some basic questions: What do the instruments sound like? What roles do they have in the music? How much do they cost? What would you be able to do with each one after this year? Gather some facts. Then . . .

DO picture both choices. Be realistic.

It will take a while to get the breathing on the clarinet. But there's technique to learn with drums, too.

DON'T be overly wishful or overly negative.

Drums should be super easy. I can play them the first day. The clarinet looks hard. I'll never be able to do it.

DO decide what's most important to you.

I want to be able to play tunes on my own.

DON'T get lost in the information.

I can think of 25 reasons to play each instrument. Can I think of 50?

DO listen to *you*.

Drums are fun, but I love holding a clarinet.

DON'T listen to peer pressure.

Are clarinets just weird? My friends will think playing drums is cooler.

DO accept that there's a bit of a gamble in every choice.

> Playing the clarinet might be really hard or it might not.

DON'T spin out over things you can't control or try to predict the future.

> What if I'm the only girl? How can I figure out what it will be like? I just want to KNOW.

DO accept that there are pros and cons to both. You'll gain some things and lose others.

> I have to choose.

DON'T think you can have it all.

> I want to play both.

DO ask: What's best for me in the long run?

DON'T ask: What's safest and easiest?

> Drums seem easier.

> I could play drums in a rock band in high school. I could play the clarinet in band or orchestra. Both would be fun.

DO keep perspective.

> If I don't like playing the clarinet, I can always drop it.

DON'T make it more important than it is.

> If I choose wrong, I'll hate it. I'll play horribly, and people will laugh. I'll flunk.

DO take action.

> OK. Clarinet.

DON'T freeze up.

> What if I make the wrong decision?

And perhaps the most important thing of all? **DON'T** keep reliving a decision once you've made it.

Was this the right decision?
Was this the right decision?
Was this the right decision?

LET IT GO.

> That's done. Now I start practicing.

getting those zzz's

Sleep is key for girls who worry. When you don't get enough sleep, you're more irritable. You're more prone to worry. And when you worry, it's harder to get to sleep. It doesn't help that sleep may get more challenging around this age.

Why does it? Your body's natural sleep times tend to shift as you go through puberty. For many kids, this means not being ready to sleep until later at night—and not feeling fully awake until midmorning. You probably can't undo this natural change. But there's a lot you can do about other reasons you may wake up groggy and grumpy.

I have a problem going to sleep on time. I just lie awake in my bed. I finally fall asleep but then wake up late for school.
—Sleep Deprived

Turn off all screens at least an hour before bed. That bluish glow makes your brain act like it's daytime.

Steer clear of chocolate and drinks with caffeine in them. They rev up your body unnaturally.

Get exercise and time outdoors each day. Just as exercise relieves stress, it also paves the way for sleep. A little sunlight keeps your body in tune with the right times for being awake and asleep.

Make bed a peaceful place. Say no to homework in bed, yes to happy photos on the nightstand, yes to comfy jammies, and yes to a beloved stuffie if you have one.

Aim to get up about the same time every day if you can—even on weekends. Sleeping in only makes it harder to get to sleep later. Your body wants to follow a regular sleep schedule.

Still can't sleep? Don't keep struggling! Nothing steals sleep faster than fretting about it. Just resting is good for your body, too. So let yourself lie quietly. Draw soothing patterns. Read a not-too-intense story. Practice deep breathing. If something's bugging you, make a list of things you could do about it once you get up. Then picture yourself setting the worry down like a heavy package. You don't need to carry it for now.

NERVOUS ABOUT THE NEWS

What if the kinds of things you worry about are big, scary things—the things you hear about in the news? The headlines can make the world seem like a very dangerous, worrisome place. But there are a lot of other things you don't usually see in the news. Knowing these facts can make the headlines easier to handle.

Scary stuff is rare.

If the news were about the things that happen most often, the headlines would be very different: Kids Go to School and Do Homework! People Watch TV! Neighbors Help One Another! But of course that's not how the news works. Most news is news because it doesn't happen very often, and it's very, very unlikely to happen to you.

You are safe.

Talk with your parents or teachers about what you've heard. They can help you understand all the ways they're looking out for your safety. They can also remind you of things *you* can do to keep yourself safe. If news about a fire bothers you, for example, you can practice what to do in case of a fire at home.

There is lots of good.

For every one person who does something bad or gets hurt, there are countless firefighters, doctors, nurses, teachers, police officers, religious leaders, and other adults who are doing lots of good in the world. When you read or hear about a bad event, pay attention to all the people who are helping others or working to make the situation better. They're everywhere, even if the news doesn't focus on them.

Kids can make a difference.

You can help, too, when bad things happen. You can help raise money to solve a problem. You can send cards to people who have been hurt. You can write letters so leaders will pay attention. When you are busy helping, there's less room in your head for worry.

HELP WANTED

NEEDED: One regular girl

JOB: Speaking out and lending a hand

PAY: Feeling Awesome!

LEMONADE SAVE THE ANIMALS

the world outside your worry

Want to win against worry? Try a little kindness.

In lots of situations, you can melt your own worries just by being kind to someone else. How does it work? Let's say you worry a lot about fitting in—about whether others will like you or accept you. Or perhaps you get really nervous when you meet new people. Does that sound familiar? If so, the next time you start a new class or join a team or go to a party, think about this choice . . .

You can dwell on your own fear.

You can spend your energy worrying about what other people think of you. You can try every way possible to avoid talking to anyone new. You can slink home afterward feeling exhausted and maybe even bad about yourself because no one seemed to like you.

Or you can try an experiment.

Instead of getting caught up in your own doubts, you can focus on how some of the other kids in the room might be feeling. Chances are, at least a few of them are worried, too. You could pick someone who looks uncomfortable and ask her questions. Really tune in to her answers. You could put your energy into helping her feel at ease. And, guess what? You may be surprised to find that *you* feel better, too.

In almost any situation there are opportunities to break free from that laser focus on your own anxious feelings. Looking for small ways to be helpful or friendly—opening a door, holding a package, offering someone a piece of gum—is a super way to start.

You can also throw your nervous energy into volunteer projects. Help sort food at the local food bank. Join the school welcome committee and give tours to new kids. Form a "raking brigade" with your friends to clear leaves for elderly neighbors. The moment you shift your attention and energy away from your worries, a whole new world will open up around you.

so, really, what if?

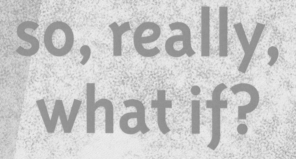

I don't want to deprive myself of fun anymore. This is something I figured out when I started to challenge myself.

—Kena

making friends with maybe

For a girl who worries, one of the hardest things is just not knowing what will happen—those times when "maybe" is the only answer to her questions.

Will I make a friend like Marco at my new school?
Will Jiaying be mad at me if I tell her how I feel?
Will I make the A team in soccer tryouts?

Girls who are uncomfortable with uncertainty tend to spend a huge amount of time and energy trying to avoid it. They steer clear of new people. *What if that kid turns out to be weird—or mean?* They dodge invitations to try new things. *What if I don't like curry?* They might make a lot of lists and try to plan every moment of a day so that nothing is left to chance.

But trying to eliminate uncertainty is a recipe for misery because it's just not possible. So what if you look at "maybe" in a different way?

Do you like it when someone reveals the entire plot of a movie you haven't seen? Do you enjoy a book if you're able to predict what's going to happen next? Knowing everything in advance can drain the fun right out of any story. That's why people call it a "spoiler" when someone gives too much away.

Your life has a story, too. Having to wonder how each chapter will turn out can be uncomfortable sometimes. But a story without any "maybes" at all won't have much excitement. "Maybe" gives you possibilities. "Maybe" keeps you curious. "Maybe" means your life is not a textbook or a form that's already been filled out—it's an adventure that you're writing as you go. "Maybe" is what makes your story fun.

go for it!

You've got the knowledge about how worry works. You've got the mental tools to combat it. You know how to face a fear and how to make daily life less stressful. You've even got some tricks that will help you make peace with "maybe." Put it all together, and soon you'll find that worry isn't holding you back anymore.

What do you do now?

Whatever you like.

What's something you've always wanted to do?
What's a dream you've always had?
What hope is inside you waiting to come out?

Here I am! I'm so glad I didn't let worry stop me.

I think I will . . .

Set your sights and go for it.

Sing in front of strangers.

Learn Chinese.

Raise your hand in class.

Get a new haircut.

Swim in your first race.

Make a mistake and keep going.

Learn to ski.

Say what you think at lunch.

Confront a bully.

A world of choices is open to you. And why?

93

Because
worry's not
in charge
anymore.

YOU are.

How's it going?

Write to us and tell us how you're doing with your worries. What's helping you take charge of them? What advice do you have for girls like you? How has your life gotten better? We'd love to know.

Write to
***Worry* Editor**
American Girl
8400 Fairway Place
Middleton, WI 53562

All comments and suggestions received by American Girl may be used without compensation or acknowledgment. We're sorry—we're unable to return photos.

Answer: What did the authors do on purpose on pages 54–55? They named the list "10 Reasons" but gave only 9!

Here are some other American Girl books you might like:

Each sold separately. Find more books online at americangirl.com.

Parents, request a FREE catalog at **americangirl.com/catalog**.
Sign up at **americangirl.com/email** to receive the latest news and exclusive offers.

Discover online games, quizzes, activities,
and more at **americangirl.com**